ST. LOUIS GATEWAY ARCH

Keli Sipperley

Rourke
Educational Media

eeducationalmedia.com

Scan for Related Titles
and Teacher Resources

Before Reading:

Building Academic Vocabulary and Background Knowledge

Before reading a book, it is important to tap into what your child or students already know about the topic. This will help them develop their vocabulary, increase their reading comprehension, and make connections across the curriculum.

1. *Look at the cover of the book. What will this book be about?*
2. *What do you already know about the topic?*
3. *Let's study the Table of Contents. What will you learn about in the book's chapters?*
4. *What would you like to learn about this topic? Do you think you might learn about it from this book? Why or why not?*
5. *Use a reading journal to write about your knowledge of this topic. Record what you already know about the topic and what you hope to learn about the topic.*
6. *Read the book.*
7. *In your reading journal, record what you learned about the topic and your response to the book.*
8. *After reading the book complete the activities below.*

Content Area Vocabulary
Read the list. What do these words mean?

abundant
architecture
commerce
establish
expedition
frontiersman
keelboat
interpreter
negotiate
pioneers
republic
treaty

After Reading:

Comprehension and Extension Activity

After reading the book, work on the following questions with your child or students in order to check their level of reading comprehension and content mastery.

1. *How did Sacagawea assist Lewis and Clark? (Summarize)*
2. *Why did France decide to sell the territory known as the Louisiana Territory to the United States? (Summarize)*
3. *Why is the St. Louis Arch considered to be a symbol of freedom? (Infer)*
4. *What was the purpose of Lewis and Clark's expedition? (Summarize)*
5. *Why did Americans want to go to the West? (Asking Questions)*

Extension Activity

Create a monument for your state. What would it be? What would it represent? Where would you place this monument? Who would you dedicate this monument to? Design your monument on paper or poster board. Write a speech that you will deliver to a state committee requesting their approval to construct your suggested monument.

TABLE OF CONTENTS

A TRIBUTE TO TRAILBLAZERS

A symbol of the American spirit of discovery and growth, the St. Louis Gateway Arch is a tribute to Thomas Jefferson and the explorers and **pioneers** who shaped the American West.

Located on the west bank of the Mississippi River in St. Louis, Missouri, it is the centerpiece of the Jefferson National Memorial. The Arch stands 630 feet (189 meters) high, making it the tallest monument in the United States.

The St. Louis Gateway Arch is a symbol of western expansion.

The Jefferson National Expansion Memorial includes the Arch, the surrounding grounds, the Museum of Westward Expansion, and St. Louis' Old Courthouse, the site of the first two trials of an American slave's fight to gain freedom.

The Old Courthouse is a two block walk from the St. Louis Gateway Arch.

Dred Scott

The Dred Scott case was one of the most important cases in U.S. history. Dred Scott, an American slave, sued for his family's freedom in April 1846. The first two trials were heard at the Old Courthouse in St. Louis. The U.S. Supreme Court eventually decided the case in 1857, ruling that as slaves, or "property," the Scotts were not citizens and could not sue. The decision also allowed slavery in the West. The decision led, in part, to the start of the Civil War.

Dred Scott (1795–1858)

AMERICA SPREADS WEST

In 1803, the population of the United States was growing quickly. However, **commerce** in the young nation relied upon access to the Mississippi River, which was owned by France as part of its Louisiana Territory.

This map shows the portion of the United States that was once called the Louisiana Territory.

Thomas Jefferson, the third U.S. president, wanted access to the Mississippi River. He sent James Monroe to France to **negotiate** with French leader Napoleon Bonaparte to purchase a portion of France's stake in the land.

"All eyes, all hopes, are now fixed on you, for on the event of this mission depends the future destinies of this **republic**," President Jefferson told Monroe.

Thomas Jefferson
(1743–1826)

James Monroe
(1758–1831)

Napoleon Bonaparte
(1769–1821)

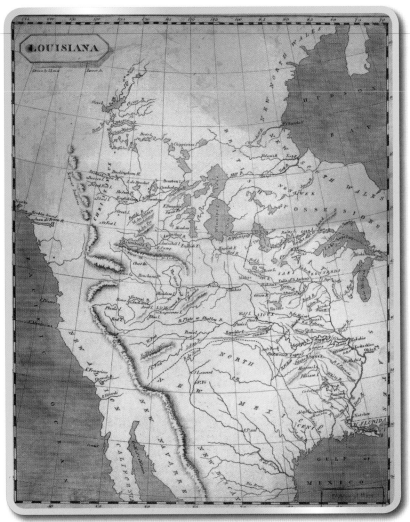

When Monroe reached France, Bonaparte refused to sell his territory to the Americans. Monroe didn't give up. He continued to try and negotiate a deal. Soon, the French leader needed money for his war with England. Bonaparte offered to sell the entire Louisiana Territory to the United States.

The official announcement of the Louisiana Purchase was made on July 4, 1803.

In April 1803, the United States reached a **treaty** with France known as the Louisiana Purchase. The deal allowed the United States to purchase 828,000 square miles (1.3 million square kilometers) of land that stretched from the Mississippi River to the Rocky Mountains for $15 million.

The Louisiana Purchase greatly increased the United States' resources. Not only did the United States now have complete control of the Mississippi River, it also had access to forests, furs, and farmland. Eventually, 15 states would be formed from the Louisiana Purchase.

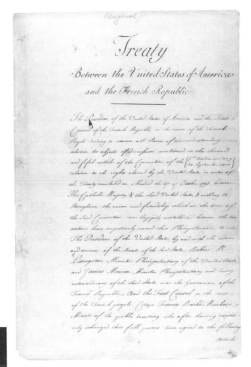

The Louisiana Purchase document.

Freedom Fact!

The Louisiana Purchase was a great bargain at about 4 cents per acre.

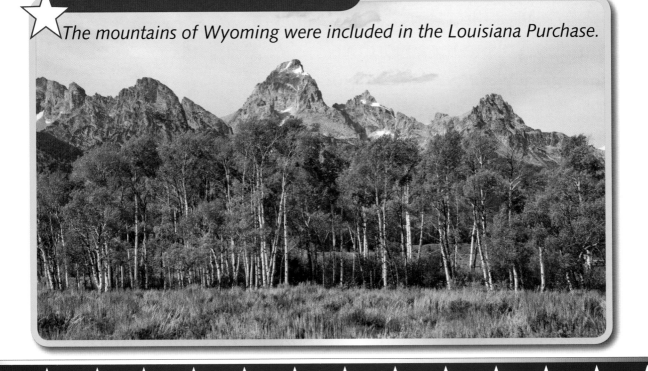

The mountains of Wyoming were included in the Louisiana Purchase.

CORPS OF DISCOVERY

Soon after the Louisiana Purchase, President Jefferson chose his personal secretary, Meriwether Lewis, to lead a special Army unit to explore the new lands. This group, called the Corps of Discovery, was also looking for a Northwest Passage: a waterway that might link the Pacific Ocean with the Mississippi River system.

Thomas Jefferson (1743–1826)

Lewis selected Army officer William Clark, a skilled **frontiersman**, as his co-captain for the journey. Together, they gathered a group of about 50 volunteer explorers to join them for the **expedition**. The Corps embarked from Camp Wood, near St. Louis, Missouri, in the summer of 1804.

The Corps began the first leg of the journey up the Missouri River aboard a 55 foot (17 meter) **keelboat** and two smaller canoes. However, the boats were not for passengers. Mostly, the boats carried the large amount of gear and supplies including food, medicine, scientific instruments, and weapons. They also carried presents of cloth, beads, tobacco, and other goods to trade with Native Americans.

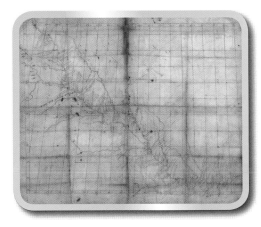

The Corps used this map to navigate part of their journey.

Between 1804 and 1806, the Corps traveled more than 8,000 miles (12,800 kilometers) on horseback, on foot, and in boats.

This is a replica of the keelboat used the Corps of Discovery.

Members of the Corps studied the landscape and its natural resources. They described **abundant** wildlife found in the territory. They wrote about the plants, animals, and mineral resources in great depth. Clark drew intricate maps that noted rivers and creeks. He also detailed the shapes of the rivers' shores.

Lewis and Clark consult with Sacagawea, a young Native American, who served as an interpreter for the expedition.

In addition to charting the new territory, President Jefferson asked Lewis and Clark to **establish** relationships with Native Americans tribes. The Corps offered the Native Americans gifts and spoke with the tribe leaders. They requested peace between tribes in the area and promised trading opportunities with the United States.

Most of the tribes the explorers encountered welcomed the group. The Native Americans provided the Corps members with food, guides, and shelter. A young Native American woman named Sacagawea became a member of the Corps of Discovery when her husband, Toussaint Charbonneau, became the group's **interpreter**.

Sacagawea

A member of the Shoshoni tribe, Sacagawea was 16 years old and the mother of a newborn son when she set out with the Corps. Sacagawea helped by digging roots, gathering food, and teaching the men to make leather clothes and moccasins.

Sacagawea (1788 – death unknown)

The Lewis and Clark expedition made a triumphant return to St. Louis, Missouri, on September 23, 1806, marking the first recorded overland, round-trip journey from the Mississippi River to the Pacific Coast.

"In obedience to your orders we have penetrated the Continent of North America to the Pacific Ocean," Lewis wrote to President Jefferson.

The explorers' return was met with jubilation from the American people, who had not heard anything of the Corps' whereabouts in more than a year. Before their return, some feared the group had perished.

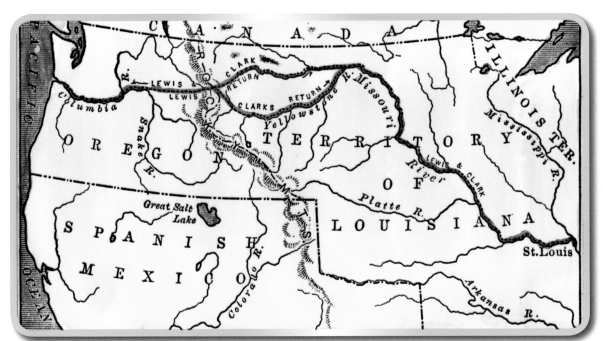

Lewis, Clark, and their fellow explorers traveled from St. Louis to the Pacific Ocean.

The expedition was a great achievement. The Corps had traveled through unknown and wild land. When they returned to St. Louis, the

Freedom Fact!

To Jefferson's disappointment, the Corps did not find a direct water route to the Pacific. There is no Northwest Passage.

expedition had successfully charted an overland route to the Pacific Ocean. This route would become a pathway for the United States to spread westward, from sea to shining sea. It is one of the greatest adventures in American history.

William Clark's journal included sketches of the wildlife they encountered, such as this evergreen shrub leaf.

15

ST. LOUIS BECOMES THE GATEWAY

St. Louis, the site of the expedition's return, is nestled just below the Missouri River's entrance into the Mississippi. Its location made it the ideal starting point for the many expeditions into the West.

The city, which was originally founded as a fur trading post in 1764, became a hub for pioneers as they set out to explore and settle the West. For many, St. Louis was the last place they could gather supplies before starting on the westward trail blazed by Lewis and Clark. The bustling city had become the Gateway to the West.

This painting by Fernand LeQuesne illustrates the founding of St. Louis in 1764. The painting, which includes angels overseeing the new city, is an example of the way many imagined the settlement of the West.

But by 1933, with the days of westward expansion behind, the city's riverfront had become neglected. Luckily, a prominent attorney and civic leader, Luther Ely Smith, had an idea to restore St. Louis. As Smith was returning from a visit to a memorial in Indiana, his train passed the rundown riverfront. He thought a memorial would revitalize the area and give the city's economy a much-needed boost.

Smith got St. Louis Mayor Bernard Dickmann on board with the idea. Then, with the approval of city leaders, the Jefferson National Expansion Memorial Association was created.

The association's goal was to create a public memorial to the men who made the western territorial expansion possible.

The focus of the memorial association was President Jefferson, who had championed westward expansion. But it was also intended to pay tribute to Lewis and Clark and the "hardy hunters, trappers, frontiersmen, and pioneers who contributed to the territorial expansion and development of these United States."

St. Louis had fallen into disrepair by the early 1930s. Luther Ely Smith wanted to restore the area by building a memorial.

The development of the memorial was not a speedy undertaking. The association worked hard to raise money and start building. But, when the United States entered World War II in 1941, the memorial was put on hold.

During World War II, planning for the St. Louis memorial stopped.

After the war, plans got underway again. A competition for the monument's design was announced in 1947. Plenty of architects and engineers were thrilled with the idea of designing this important monument. And with the war over, many Americans were eager for this project to get underway and supported its construction.

Warehouses along the river were demolished to make room for the riverfront memorial.

More than 145 people entered their designs for the memorial. But it was Finnish-American architect Eero Saarinen's design that stood out. His monument featured a 630 foot (189 meter) stainless steel arch towering over the Mississippi River. It captured the imagination of the judges and the spirit of the Gateway.

Eero Saarinen
(1910–1961)

Saarinen's passion for **architecture** began as a child, and he came by it naturally. His father, Eliel Saarinen, also was an architect. In fact, both father and son submitted designs for the memorial.

The family just learned that Eero's design had made it to the second round and were still in the midst of celebrating that achievement when they were notified that his design had won. Eero's arch would be the monument to the West.

"Here, at the edge of the Mississippi River, a great arch did seem right," Eero Saarinen said.

On a clear day, visitors can see up to 30 miles (48 kilometers) away from the observation room at the top of the Arch.

Land for the Jefferson National Expansion Memorial was dedicated on June 10, 1950, by President Harry S. Truman. But the project was once again delayed by the onset of another battle, the Korean War.

President Truman (1884–1972)

Construction of the Arch cost more than $13.4 million.

Sadly, Eero Saarinen did not live to see his vision realized. The architect died September 1, 1961. Construction of the Gateway Arch got underway in 1963. Two years later, the last section was put into place on October 28, 1965. It opened to the public on July 24, 1967.

HOW TO VISIT

The Gateway Arch attracts millions of visitors every year. If you visit, you can ride a tram up to the viewing center. At the top of the Arch there are 16 windows on each side. On a clear day, you can see up to 30 miles (48 kilometers) out in either direction!

The trams travel 340 feet (103 meters) per minute, which is about 3.86 miles per hour (6.2 kilometers per hour). It takes about four minutes to reach the top of the Arch from the base. The viewing area at the top can hold up to 160 people.

Freedom Fact!

- It weighs 17,246 tons (15,645 metric tons).
- Its foundations extend 60 feet (18 meters) into the ground.
- Crews used 900 tons (816 metric tons) of stainless steel to build the Arch, more than any project in history.
- Built to withstand earthquakes and high winds, the Arch can sway up to 18 inches (46 centimeters).

In addition to seeing the Arch, you also can explore the other areas of the Jefferson National Expansion Memorial. The Museum of Westward Expansion displays artifacts from the Lewis and Clark expedition, as well as an authentic American Indian tipi.

You can start your tour at the visitor's center.

The Old Courthouse, where the two trials of the important Dred Scott case were held, is also part of the Memorial. It is one of the oldest standing buildings in St. Louis. You can also embark on a cruise to explore the Mississippi River, just as Lewis and Clark did more than 200 years ago.

The Gateway Arch rises behind the Old Courthouse.

TIMELINE

1764 —— *French fur trader Pierre Laclède Liguest founds St. Louis.*

1804 —— *The Louisiana Purchase is made, and the Corps of Discovery begin their expedition.*

1806 —— *St. Louis becomes known as the Gateway to the West when Lewis and Clark return.*

1847 —— *The first Dred Scott case is tried at the Old Courthouse.*

1935 —— *The Jefferson National Expansion Memorial becomes a national park.*

1941 —— *The United States enters World War II, delaying the Jefferson memorial project.*

1947 —— *Finnish-American architect Eero Saarinen's design wins the contest.*

1950 —— *Harry S. Truman dedicates land for the memorial. The project is again put on hold due to the Korean War.*

1961 —— *Eero Saarinen dies on September 1.*

1963 —— *Construction of the Arch begins.*

1965 —— *The Arch is completed on October 28.*

1967 —— *The Arch opens to public on July 24.*

GLOSSARY

abundant (uh-BUHN-duhnt): having a great amount of something; having more than enough

architecture (AHR-ki-tek-chur): the art or practice of designing and building structures

commerce (KAH-murs): the exchange or buying and selling of goods on a large scale involving transportation from place to place

establish (ih-STAB-lish): to start or make stable

expedition (ek-spuh-DISH-uhn): a journey or excursion undertaken for a specific purpose

frontiersman (fruhn-TEERS-man): a person who lives or works on a frontier

interpreter (in-TUR-pri-tur): someone whose job is to translate from one language to another

keelboat (keel-boht): a shallow, covered riverboat used for freight that is usually rowed, poled, or towed

negotiate (ni-GOH-shee-eyt): to make a deal or bargain

pioneers (pye-uh-NEERS): a group of people that originates or helps open up a new line of thought or activity; one of the first to settle in a territory

republic (ri-PUHB-lik): a government having a chief of state who is not a monarch and who in modern times is usually a president

treaty (TREE-tee): a contract in writing between two or more political authorities formally signed by authorized representatives

INDEX

SHOW WHAT YOU KNOW

1. Why is the Louisiana Purchase considered one of President Thomas Jefferson's greatest achievements?
2. How did the Lewis and Clark expedition contribute to the expansion of the American West?
3. Why was St. Louis chosen as the location for the Jefferson National Expansion Memorial?
4. For what reasons was construction of the Arch delayed?
5. What did Luther Ely Smith hope a memorial on the riverbank in St. Louis would do for the city?

WEBSITES TO VISIT

www.nps.gov/jeff/index.htm

www.gatewayarch.com

www.lewisandclarktrail.com

ABOUT THE AUTHOR

Keli Sipperley is a multimedia journalist and children's book author in Tampa, Florida. She enjoys writing stories about interesting moments, fun places, and people who help others in their communities. She has two sons and two daughters who love reading and writing as much as she does.

Meet The Author!
www.meetREMauthors.com

© 2015 Rourke Educational Media

www.rourkeeducationalmedia.com

PHOTO CREDITS: Cover © semmick Photo; title page © Gino Santa Maria; top bar © rudi1976; page 4 © kubrak78; pae 5 © National Park Service, picturehistory.com; page 6 © ErnsstA; page 7, 10, 11, 13, 24 © Library of Congress, Samuel Morse (1791-1872), Jacques-Louis David (1748-1825); page 8 © pearley; page 9 © National Archives, Jeff Goulden; page 11 © keelboat.com; page 12 © The Granger Collection, New York; page 14, 15 © North Wind Pictures Archive; page 17 © Fernand Le Qiesne (1856-1932); 20 © US Army; page 21 © Jefferson National Expansion Memorial Archives; page 22 © AP/Corbis/ Bettman; page 23 © Daniel Sohwen; page 24 © AP/Fred Waters 1965; page 25 © Sterling E. Stevens; page 27 © Matthew hoelscher, Rudy Balsko

Edited by: Jill Sherman

Cover design by: Nicola Stratford, nicolastratford.com
Interior design by: Renee Brady

Library of Congress PCN Data

St. Louis Gateway Arch / Keli Sipperley
(Symbols of Freedom)
ISBN 978-1-62717-742-9 (hard cover)
ISBN 978-1-62717-864-8 (soft cover)
ISBN 978-1-62717-975-1 (e-Book)
Library of Congress Control Number: 2014935668
Printed in the United States of America, North Mankato, Minnesota

Also Available as: